KOUZES
POSNER

JOSSEY-BASS
A Wiley Imprint
www.josseybass.com

Published by Jossey-Bass
A Wiley Imprint
989 Market Street, San Francisco, CA 94103-1741
www.josseybass.com

Jossey-Bass books and products are available through most
bookstores. To contact Jossey-Bass directly call our
Customer Care Department within the U.S. at 800-956-7739,
outside the U.S. at 317-572-3986 or fax 317-572-4002.
Jossey-Bass also publishes its books in a variety of electronic
formats. Some content that appears in print may not be
available in electronic books.

Printed in the United States of America
first edition
ISBN 0-7879-6822-6
PB Printing   10   9   8   7   6   5   4   3   2   1

Alan —

Happy Birthday

and may all your

days be full of

wonderment.

Your Friend.

ALSO BY JIM KOUZES AND BARRY POSNER

The Leadership Challenge
Credibility
Encouraging the Heart
The Leadership Challenge Workbook
Leadership Practices Inventory (LPI), 3rd Edition
LPI Online
The Jossey-Bass Academic Administrator's Guide
to Exemplary Leadership
Student Leadership Practices Inventory (Student LPI)

To learn more about these publications, please visit
www.leadershipchallenge.com

Introduction

THE LEADERSHIP CHALLENGE JOURNAL IS INTENDED to engage you in reflecting on the joys and struggles of leadership. Reflection is not something we do often enough. Our days are too full. We're too busy. There's just too much to *do*.

But not taking time to reflect on our lives as leaders is like not taking time to look in the mirror in the morning. We wouldn't think of not checking at least briefly to make sure of our outer image. But what about checking out what's inside? What about our *inner* image?

Taking time to reflect is essential to preparing ourselves to embrace the day. It's a tune-up for the soul. So as you walk along your journey's path, stop every now and then to reflect.

Think of *The Leadership Challenge Journal* as your companion and your guide. Use it to take notes, make comments, draw pictures, get organized, give answers, ask questions, ponder, or just meditate. It's meant to be a place where you can capture an inspiration, reveal a truth, express an emotion, or record a challenge.

Whether you're an experienced or an aspiring leader, we invite you to take *The Leadership Challenge Journal* along with you on your leadership adventures. Let it be a place of comfort and serenity in times of turmoil and disquiet, a catalyst for uplifting your spirits when you experience uncertainty and doubt, and a setting for readying yourself to make a difference.

Hang on to this journal. You can return to it again and again. One of the things we've learned is that people who keep journals do far better in times of transition than those who don't.

We wish you continuing joy and success on your journey to becoming a better leader.

Leaders

BEYOND THE HORIZON OF TIME IS A CHANGED WORLD. A world different from today's world.

Some people see across this boundary of experience and into the future. They believe that dreams can become realities. They open our eyes and lift our spirits. They build our trust and strengthen our relationships. They stand firm against the winds of resistance and give us courage to continue the quest.

We call them leaders. They take us to places we have never been before. We are fortunate that they do.

_____

_____

_____

✳ | More than ever
there is need for
people to seize the
opportunities to lead
us to greatness.

_____

_____

_____

_____

_____

_____

_____

_____

_____

_____

_____

_____

_____

_____

_____

_____

_____

✳ | Leadership begins
with something that
grabs hold of you
and won't let go.

✳ | Leadership is every-
one's business.

We make extraordinary things happen when we liberate the leader within everyone.

The domain of
leaders is the
future. The leader's
unique legacy
is the creation of
valued institutions
that stand the test
of time.

The most significant contribution leaders make is not simply to today's bottom line; it is to the long-term development of people and institutions so they can adapt, change, prosper, and grow.

We all want to know
that we've done
something special
on this earth, that
there's a purpose to
our existence.

Model the Way

EXEMPLARY LEADERS STAND FOR SOMETHING, believe in something, and care about something. They *find their voice* by clarifying their personal values and then expressing those values in their own unique and authentic style. Leaders also know they cannot force their views on others. Instead, they work tirelessly to forge consensus around a set of common principles.

Eloquent speeches about admirable beliefs, however, aren't nearly enough. Words and deeds must be consistent for leaders to have integrity. Leaders must *set the example* by aligning their personal actions with shared values. When constituents know that their leaders have the courage of convictions, they are more willing to commit. People first follow the person, then the plan.

* The quest for lead-
ership is first an
inner quest to dis-
cover who you are.

_____

_____

_____

_____

_____

_____

_____

_____

_____

_____

_____

_____

_____

_____

_____

_____

_____

_____

_____

_____

_____

_____

_____

_____

_____

_____

_____

_____

_____

_____

_____

_____

_____

_____

_____

⁂ | You can't have the
courage of your
convictions if you
have no convictions.

_____

_____

_____

When you give voice
to the principles that
govern your life, you
give purpose to your
daily actions.

If you don't find your
authentic voice,
you'll end up with
a vocabulary that
belongs to someone
else.

_____

_____

_____

_____

_____

_____

_____

_____

_____

_____

_____

_____

_____

_____

_____

_____

_____

_____

_____

_____

_____

> If people don't
> believe *in* the
> messenger, they
> won't believe the
> message.

✳ | Leadership is a
dialogue, not a
monologue.

_____

_____

_____

_____

_____

＊ For people to under-
stand and come to
agree with values,
they must partici-
pate in the process;
*unity is forged, not
forced.*

The legacy you
leave is the life
you lead.

The behavior that is
modeled becomes
the behavior that
is followed.

Titles are granted.
It's your behavior
that earns you
respect.

Inspire a
Shared Vision

THERE IS NO FREEWAY TO THE FUTURE. No paved highway from here to tomorrow. There is only wilderness. Only uncertain terrain. There are no roadmaps. No signposts. Pioneering leaders rely on a compass and a dream.

Leaders *envision the future* by imagining exciting and ennobling possibilities. They dream of what might be, and they passionately believe that they can make a positive difference.

But visions seen only by the leader are insufficient to mobilize and energize. Leaders *enlist others* in exciting possibilities by appealing to shared aspirations. They breathe life into ideal and unique images of the future and get others to see how their own dreams can be realized by embracing a common vision.

_____

_____

_____

✳ | All endeavors, big or   _____
small, begin in the
mind's eye.   _____

_____

_____

_____

_____

_____

_____

_____

_____

_____

_____

_____

_____

_____

_____

———————————————————————————————

———————————————————————————————

———————————————————————————————

———————————————————————————————

———————————————————————————————

———————————————————————————————

———————————————————————————————

———————————————————————————————

———————————————————————————————

———————————————————————————————

———————————————————————————————

———————————————————————————————

———————————————————————————————

※ | Are you in your job
to do something, or
are you in your job
for something to do?

———————————————————————————————

———————————————————————————————

———————————————————————————————

✳ | Leaders breathe
life into visions.

---

* Leadership is not
about selling *your*
dream; it's about
creating a *shared*
sense of destiny.

Great leaders
create meaning,
not just make
money.

✳ Leaders find the common thread that weaves the fabric of human needs into a colorful tapestry.

Constituents don't serve leaders; leaders serve constituents. Both serve a common purpose.

Leaders cannot
command
commitment,
only inspire it.

Enlisting in a vision
of the future is like
putting together a
jigsaw puzzle. It's a
lot easier when you
can see the picture
on the box top.

Challenge the Process

THE WORK OF LEADERS IS CHANGE. To them the status quo is unacceptable. Leaders *search for opportunities* by seeking innovative ways to change, grow, and improve. They seize the initiative to make things happen. And knowing they have no monopoly on good ideas, leaders constantly scan the outside environment for creative ways to do new things.

You can't get from here to tomorrow in one giant leap. Extraordinary things don't get done one step at a time. Leaders *experiment and take risks* by constantly generating small wins and by learning from mistakes. And, despite persistent opposition and inevitable setbacks, leaders demonstrate the courage to continue the quest.

_____

_____

_____

✳ No one ever used   _____

    the word *boring* to
    describe a personal   _____

    best leadership
    experience.   _____

    Humdrum situations
    simply aren't   _____

    associated with
    award-winning   _____

    performances.
                              _____

_____

_____

_____

_____

_____

_____

_____

_____

_____

_____

✳ | Challenge is the
opportunity for
greatness.

It's not so important whether you find the challenges or they find you. What *is* important are the choices you make when stuff happens.

_____

_____

_____

_____

_____

_____

_____

_____

_____

_____

_____

_____

_____

_____

Adversity brings us
face-to-face with
who we really are
and what we're
capable of
becoming.

_____

_____

_____

_____

✳ | The question is:
When opportunity
knocks are you
prepared to open
the door?

*Instill a sense of adventure in everything you do. Instill a sense of wonder in the people who do it.

Great ideas never
enter the mind
through an open
mouth.

Small wins generate
momentum, attract
constituents, build
confidence, and
keep people focused
on the road ahead.

Leaders have their
heads in the clouds,
and their feet on
the ground. That
way they can still
envision the summit,
but ascend it by put-
ting one foot in front
of the other.

Leaders don't look
for someone to
blame when
mistakes are made
in the name of
innovation. Instead,
they ask, "What can
be learned from the
experience?

Enable Others to Act

LEADERS KNOW THEY CAN'T DO IT ALONE. It takes partners to get extraordinary things done in organizations. So, leaders *foster collaboration* by promoting cooperative goals and building trust. They develop teams with spirit and cohesion. They promote a sense of reciprocity and a feeling of "we're all in this together."

Leaders understand that mutual respect is what sustains extraordinary efforts. Leaders *strengthen others* by sharing power and providing choice, making each person feel competent and confident. They nurture self-esteem and sustain human dignity.

_____

_____

_____

✳ | "You can't do it   _____
    alone," is the
    mantra of   _____
    exemplary leaders.
                       _____

_____

_____

_____

_____

_____

_____

_____

_____

_____

_____

_____

_____

Pursuing excellence
is a collaborator's
game.

Trust is the glue
that binds
relationships.

✳ | Leaders make peo-
ple feel like owners,
not just hired hands.

_____

_____

_____

* Today's critical
currency isn't
intellectual or
economic capital
but *social capital*—
the collective value
of the people we
know and what we'll
do for each other.

_____

_____

_____

_____

_____

_____

_____

_____

_____

_____

_____

_____

_____

_____

_____

_____

_____

_____

_____

_____

_____

_____

_____

_____

_____

_____

_____

_____

_____

_____

_____

_____

_____

_____

_____

_____

Demonstrate trust *in*
others before asking
for trust *from* others.

The simple act of
listening is a
profound act
of respect.

The paradox of power is that we become most powerful when we give our own power away.

Leaders turn their
constituents into
leaders.

Encourage the Heart

THE CLIMB TO THE TOP IS ARDUOUS AND STEEP.
People become exhausted, frustrated, and
disenchanted. They're tempted to give up.

To keep hope and determination alive, leaders
recognize contributions by showing appreciation
for individual excellence. Genuine acts of
caring uplift spirits and strengthen courage.

On every winning team, the members need to
share in the rewards of their efforts. So leaders
celebrate the values and the victories by creating a
spirit of community. They express pride in the
accomplishments of their team, and they make
everyone feel like everyday heroes.

✳ | Caring is at the
heart of leadership.
Without caring,
leadership has
no soul.

＊ It is often the simple,
personal gestures
that are the most
powerful rewards.

_____

_____

_____

_____

_____

_____

_____

_____

_____

_____

_____

_____

✳ | Recognition is   _____
    feedback. People
    need to know if   _____
    they're making
    progress toward the   _____
    goal, not simply
    marking time.   _____

                             _____

_____

_____

_____

✳ | It is not what gets
rewarded that gets
done; it's what *is*
rewarding that
gets done.

With a thank you note, a smile, and public praise, leaders let others know how much they mean to the organization.

Stories put a human
face on success.
They tell us that
someone just like us
can make it happen.

Listen with your
eyes and hearts
and not just your
ears and brain.

Knowing that we
aren't alone and that
we can count on
others helps build
the courage to con-
tinue in the quest.

Celebrations are
much more than
parties; they're
ceremonies and
rituals that create
meaning.

Leadership Is Personal

IN THE END, LEADERSHIP DEVELOPMENT is ultimately self-development. It's pure myth that only a lucky few can ever understand the intricacies of leadership. Leadership is not a place, it's not a gene, and it's not a secret code that can't be deciphered by ordinary people.

The truth is that leadership is an observable set of skills and abilities that are useful whether one is in the executive suite or on the front line, on Wall Street or Main Street, in any campus, community, or corporation.

Meeting the Leadership Challenge is a personal—and a daily challenge—for all of us.

✳ | If *we* are to become
leaders, we must
believe that we can
be a positive force
in the world.

✳ | Learning to lead
    changes who you are. _____

✳ We *become* leaders;
we don't just *do*
leadership.

Leaders aren't
saints. They're
human beings, full
of the flaws and
failings of the rest
of us. They make
mistakes.

Humility is the only
way to resolve the
conflicts and
contradictions of
leadership.

Leaders
stay in love.

Leadership is *not* an affair of the head. Leadership is an affair of the heart.

The Journey Continues

THE WORDS JOURNAL AND JOURNEY have the same root. They both derive from the word meaning *a day*.

Much of what we know about great expeditions is what the explorers recorded at the end of a day. It's because they took the time to reflect on what had happened, how they felt, and what it all meant that we are able to learn and appreciate what it's like to be inside the hearts and minds of adventurers.

So, too, with you. Your capacity to learn, grow, and move on will be significantly enhanced if you continue to reflect on, record, and relate the stories of your daily adventures. Your capacity to become a better leader flows from your experience. And experience can be the best teacher if you pause long enough to reflect on it. It's not the experience that counts, but what you get out of the experience.

And the journey never ends. The sun will set on today's travels, and the sun will rise on tomorrow's opportunities. When the sun sets on your day, capture the learning. When the sun rises again, seize the opportunity to make a difference.

Leadership matters. People matter. You matter.